TAKE ACTION SAVE ON EARTH

T0102564

SAVE POLLINATORS

Stephanie Feldstein

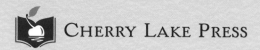

Published in the United States of America by Cherry Lake Publishing Group
Ann Arbor, Michigan
www.cherrylakepublishing.com

Reading Adviser: Beth Walker Gambro, MS, Ed., Reading Consultant, Yorkville, IL
Book Designer: Felicia Macheske

Photo Credits: © ulrich missbach/Shutterstock, cover; © irin-k/Shutterstock, 5, back cover; © Nella/Shutterstock,5; © NinaMalyna/Shutterstock, 9; Library of Congress, photographer unknown, Soldiers Wearing Gas Masks., 1918 or 1919, LOC Control No: 2016645678, 11; © IndianFaces/Shutterstock, 13; © 2009fotofriends/Shutterstock, 14; © Andry_nw/Shutterstock, 17; © smilesbevie/Shutterstock, 18; © Ana Moreno; 21; © HWK-Fotografie/Shutterstock, 23; © Chris Allan/Shutterstock, 24; © nieriss/Shutterstock, 27; © Neil Liesenfeld/Shutterstock, 29; © David Jeffrey Ringer/Shutterstock, back cover

Graphics Credits: © Pavel K/Shutterstock; © laschi/Shutterstock; © Panimoni/Shutterstock; © Hulinska Yevheniia/Shutterstock; © Vector Place/Shutterstock; © Happy Art/Shutterstock; © Peacefully7/Shutterstock; © Mushakesa/Shutterstock; © davooda/Shutterstock;

Copyright © 2024 by Cherry Lake Publishing Group

All rights reserved. No part of this book may be reproduced or utilized in any form or by any means without written permission from the publisher.

Cherry Lake Press is an imprint of Cherry Lake Publishing Group.

Library of Congress Cataloging-in-Publication Data has been filed and is available at catalog.loc.gov.

Cherry Lake Publishing Group would like to acknowledge the work of the Partnership for 21st Century Learning, a Network of Battelle for Kids. Please visit http://www.battelleforkids.org/networks/p21 for more information.

Printed in the United States of America
Corporate Graphics

Note from publisher: Websites change regularly, and their future contents are outside of our control. Supervise children when conducting any recommended online searches for extended learning opportunities.

Table of Contents

INTRODUCTION

Pollinators and the Extinction Crisis

Bumblebees have round, fuzzy bodies. The powder in the middle of flowers sticks to their tiny hairs. This powder is called pollen. It helps flowers make seeds to grow new plants. But it needs to be moved to the right part of the flower to work. That's where bumblebees come in. They beat their wings really fast. It shakes the pollen stuck to their fuzz onto other flowers. This is called **pollination**.

Pollinators are animals that move pollen between plants. There are between 200,000 and 350,000 different kinds of pollinators. Most them are insects like bees and butterflies. There are more than 20,000 kinds of bees, so scientists can't track them all.

More than one-quarter of the bumblebees in North America are in trouble. Many other kinds of pollinators are in danger, too. This is bad news for plants. And not only flowers. Trees need pollination. So does the food we grow to eat.

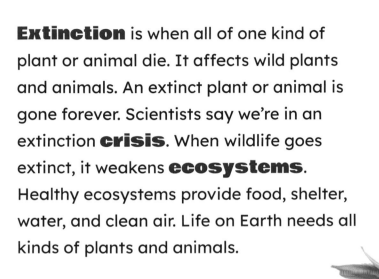

Extinction is when all of one kind of plant or animal die. It affects wild plants and animals. An extinct plant or animal is gone forever. Scientists say we're in an extinction **crisis**. When wildlife goes extinct, it weakens **ecosystems**. Healthy ecosystems provide food, shelter, water, and clean air. Life on Earth needs all kinds of plants and animals.

We can stop the extinction crisis. People like us need to take action. Governments and communities need to act, too. By working together, we can save pollinators.

Why We Need POLLINATORS

More than 80 percent of plants with flowers need pollinators to help them grow. Even giant redwood trees need pollinators. Flowering plants are important to ecosystems. Healthy plants help create soil. Their roots prevent erosion. Erosion is when the land gets worn away. This makes it harder for plants and animals to survive.

Plants that grow in the water with flowers help keep rivers and lakes clean. They make oxygen we need to breathe. They are used in medicine and cultural traditions. They can be food and shelter for other animals. They attract bugs that birds, reptiles, frogs, and other animals eat. Pollinators are important for the whole food chain.

Pollinators help feed people, too. Fruits, vegetables, nuts, and other food comes from plants with flowers. Pollinators help grow one out of every three bites of our food. Even chocolate needs pollinators.

CHAPTER ONE

Pollinators in Peril

Pollinators face many dangers. **Agriculture** needs pollinators. But it's also the biggest threat to pollinators. Agriculture is the business of how people grow crops. People have tried to find easier ways to grow more food. Companies make chemicals to kill things like weeds or bugs that farmers don't want on fields. These chemicals are called **pesticides**. But they also kill important wildlife like pollinators.

Pesticides aren't only used in agriculture. They're used in yards and gardens. They're also used by cities on parks and fields. More than 1 billion pounds (453,592,370 kilograms) of pesticides are sold in the United States every year.

Pesticides used on garden plants do not just kill "pest" insects. They also kill pollinators like bees and butterflies.

TURNING POINT

Pesticides have been used since ancient times. New ones were made during World War I (1914–1918). These pesticides were more harmful. They poisoned people and wildlife.

World War I was the first war that used chemicals as weapons. Pesticides from farms were used in the war. Research on weapons led to new pesticides. Farming and war became linked together. The United States called pesticides a "War Against Insects."

The chemicals kept getting more **toxic**. They were used for war and on crops. They poisoned water and air. People got sick. Wildlife such as pollinators died.

In 1972, the United States passed a law. It said some of the worst pesticides couldn't be used anymore. It created a way to oversee pesticides. Companies had to put warning labels on them. But more pesticides kept getting made and approved.

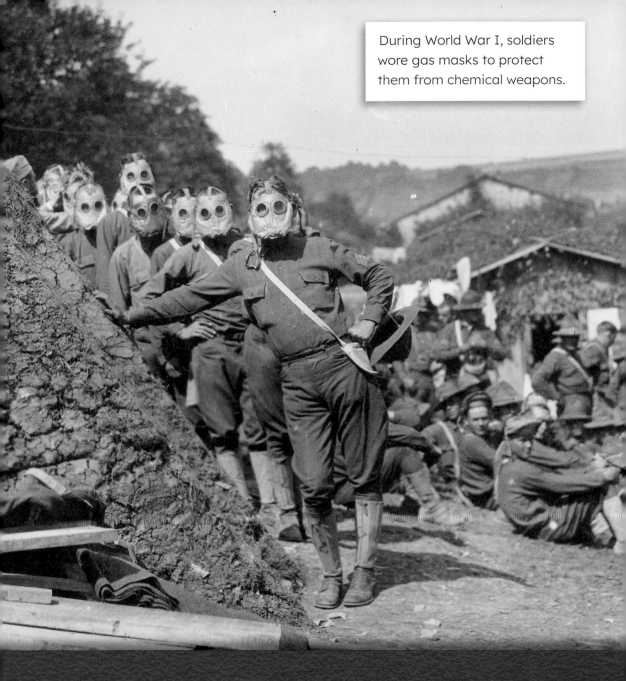

During World War I, soldiers wore gas masks to protect them from chemical weapons.

Today more than 18,000 pesticides can be used in the United States. Many of them are known to harm people and wildlife. Environmental groups are trying to change the laws to stop the use of toxic pesticides.

Pesticides are put on and near plants. They can poison pollinators. Many of the pollinators are killed right away. Some pesticides make them too weak to find food. Sometimes they can't find their nests. They get sick and die.

Monocultures make up a large share of agriculture. That means that one type of crop is grown in large fields. The most common monocultures are corn and soybeans. Pesticides are used to kill all the other kinds of plants. There's no food for pollinators to eat in these fields. There's no safe place for them to rest.

Many food labels say they're "natural." It doesn't mean what you may think. They can still be grown with pesticides. Look for "**organic**" labels. Organic foods don't use toxic chemicals. Buying organic helps pollinators and farm workers.

Habitat is the place where wild animals live. Pollinators have lost their habitats to agriculture. They've also lost it to cities and roads.

Climate change is hurting ecosystems. It causes warmer temperatures and storms. These conditions affect how plants grow. They grow at different times than they once did. This change can weaken or kill plants. Pollinators can't always find food when they need it. That also means they can't help pollinate flowers.

◀ Native prairies, like this one in Alberta, Canada, provide important natural habitat for pollinating insects.

CHAPTER TWO

Plant to Save Pollinators

Grasslands used to stretch across the United States. Some people call them prairies. They're famous for being where bison live. But they're also home to many pollinators. Grasslands are important ecosystems. Almost 75 percent of America's grasslands have disappeared. They've been replaced by agriculture and towns.

Pollinators need places to nest, sleep, and eat. They need to be safe to help plants grow. Gardens can't replace grassland habitat. But they can help create rest stops for pollinators. Together, they're like a highway to help bees and butterflies travel and find food.

Lawns are monocultures. They don't provide any food for pollinators. Some people are replacing their lawns with

Grass lawns do not provide food for pollinators. Letting clover or other flowers grow in lawns can help them survive.

Monarch butterflies travel across North American every fall. They fly thousands of miles. Eastern monarchs spend the winter in Mexico. They go back north in early spring. They need safe places to eat and rest along the way. Their caterpillars need milkweed to survive. But many of those places are now towns, roads, and farms.

People are trying to make new habitats for monarchs. They're planting milkweed in gardens. These gardens help provide food for the monarchs' long journey.

native plants and wildflowers. People who don't have yards may plant wildflowers in pots. Talk to your family about where you can start a garden. Use the tips at the end of this book to make it pollinator-friendly.

Don't use pesticides. Make sure the seeds or plants you buy weren't treated with pesticides. Ask your neighbors to stop using them, too. If they spray their plants, the chemicals can drift to your lawn and garden. Tell them why pollinators are important. Talk to them about how they can help.

Most bees don't live in hives. Most native bees nest in the ground. They dig just below the soil. Make places in your garden where bees can nest. Use compost instead of wood chips in your garden. This makes it easier for bees to nest.

Bumblebees make nests under leaves. Don't rake leaves that fall in your yard. This will help bees and your soil. Other native bees nest in hollow stems or dead wood. Add small brush piles and bits of dead wood to your garden for them. Many garden stores also have nest kits for bees in your area.

CONSERVATION CHAMPION

The Moreno Rojas family lives in a village near Cerro Pelón in Mexico. Cerro Pelón is a butterfly sanctuary. Millions of monarchs roost there every winter. The forest shelters them from the weather. Monarchs could go extinct without the sanctuary. The butterflies and the sanctuary need **conservation**. Conservation is action to protect wildlife and nature.

Ana Moreno and her brothers have been around the monarchs since they were very young. Their father was a forest ranger. He helped guard the butterflies. Ana's brother Joel started a bed and breakfast. Tourists come to visit the sanctuary and the village.

Ana and her brothers saw trees cut down every time they walked in the forest. People cut down trees to make money. But it was harming the butterflies.

Joel and Pato Moreno started a nonprofit to help the butterflies. It's called Butterflies and Their People. They hire people to guard the forest. This creates jobs for villagers. It helps local communities want to save the forest. It helps stop people from cutting down trees.

Ana Moreno left the village to study tourism in college. She wanted to learn English to share her love of monarchs with others. Now she's a butterfly guide. She takes people up the mountain to see the monarchs.

People and pollinators depend on each other. The Moreno Rojas family is creating a better future for both.

This is Joel Moreno, of the Moreno Rojas family. He is one of 10 children, all of whom contribute to Cerro Pelón monarch conservation efforts.

CHAPTER THREE

Beyond Your Backyard

Backyard gardens can't save pollinators on their own. Some pollinators need special plants. They need native habitat. Pesticides are used everywhere people grow plants. They're used on farms. They're used to make green lawns. They're used in parks and flower beds. That's why everyone needs to work together.

Cities have lots of places that can be pollinator habitat. These places include city parks and community gardens. Many buildings have flower beds. Native grasses and wildflowers can be planted next to roads. Some businesses even put gardens on their rooftops.

Many cities work with local groups to save pollinators. Together, they turn green spaces into habitat. They teach

Sunflowers, like the one this bee is on, can grow almost anywhere! They can help build up natural pollinator habitat.

Healthy pollinator gardens are good for lots of animals. The best backyard habitats use **native plants**. Harmful weeds are removed without using pesticides. The backyards have places wildlife can make a home. They have clean water for animals to drink and bathe.

Gardens can become certified habitat. That means they have all the things that make them good for wildlife. Some state wildlife agencies certify gardens. The National Wildlife Federation does, too. Certified gardens can put up a sign. The sign tells people the garden is helping wildlife. This may encourage others to create pollinator habitats in their yards.

gardeners how to help. They track what kinds of butterflies and bees are in the area.

Some companies are changing how they grow food. They create pollinator habitats on their farms. They include native plants. They use fewer pesticides. They protect pollinators from chemicals. Many farms bring in beehives to help with pollination. These companies make sure they don't hurt native bees. Companies that take all these steps can get certified. They have a Bee Better Certified label on their food. Buying Bee Better food helps pollinators.

Choosing organic food means eating foods grown without toxic chemicals. It used to be hard to find organic food. But more people have learned about pesticides. They want foods that are better for the planet and their health. Organic products are now in almost every grocery store.

SPEAK UP FOR POLLINATORS

Communities across the United States are helping protect bees. They're growing more native plants. Native plants are ones that grow naturally in an area. They're using fewer pesticides. They're teaching people how to make their gardens organic.

The Bee City USA program helps cities and towns make plans to help bees. You can ask your town to become a Bee City.

Write or email your local government officials. Tell them why pollinators are important. Talk about how pesticides hurt them. Ask them to join the Bee City USA program to make your town safe for pollinators. They can search online for "Bee City USA" to learn more.

You can also start a petition. A petition is a letter other people sign. It can show that lots of people support your cause. Gather a lot of signatures. Talk to people who

Talk to your parents or a teacher about building a bee hotel for native bees.

garden. Ask businesses to sign your petition. This shows how important pollinators are to the town. Give the petition to your mayor or town council.

Making your town safe for bees can start at school. You can ask the principal to not use pesticides. The school can plant native plants. Some schools have pollinator gardens. Ask your teacher about how your class can speak up and help.

Cows, pigs, and chickens are mostly fed corn and soybeans. These crops are usually grown as monocultures. They use a lot of pesticides. More animals raised for meat lead to more monocultures. Eating less meat can help reduce pesticides.

Some groups are working to stop pesticides from harming people and wildlife. Many pesticides have never been fully tested. We may not know all the ways they're harmful. They may be toxic to pollinators and other animals. They may pollute water. Some are known to be harmful to wildlife. The Center for Biological Diversity is a group that fights to keep these pesticides out of habitats.

Cattle are fed a lot of corn. Eating ▶ less meat means less corn is needed and fewer pesticides will be used.

ACTIVITY
CREATE A POLLINATOR GARDEN

You can give pollinators a healthy place to live. Even a small planter or flower box helps pollinators. Here's how to make a garden that pollinators will love:

1. Pick a spot in the Sun if you can. Butterflies and other pollinators like the sunshine. Many of their favorite flowers grow best in the Sun. Make sure the spot isn't too windy.

2. Choose native plants. Research what plants are native to your area. Pick a variety of different plants that pollinators like. You can buy seeds or small plants. Make sure they haven't been treated with chemicals.

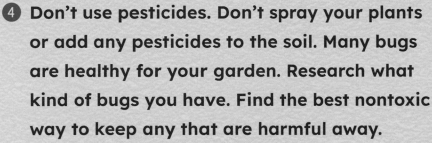

③ Prepare your garden. Mix up the soil so it's loose. Make sure it's free of grass. Add compost or potting soil. Find out the best time of year to start your garden. Some plants prefer spring. Others prefer fall. Read the instructions for your plants. Talk to an expert at your local plant nursery.

④ Don't use pesticides. Don't spray your plants or add any pesticides to the soil. Many bugs are healthy for your garden. Research what kind of bugs you have. Find the best nontoxic way to keep any that are harmful away.

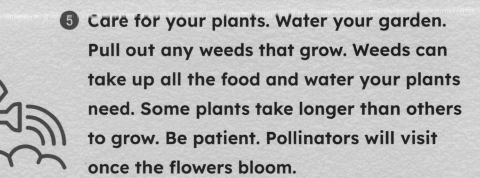

⑤ Care for your plants. Water your garden. Pull out any weeds that grow. Weeds can take up all the food and water your plants need. Some plants take longer than others to grow. Be patient. Pollinators will visit once the flowers bloom.

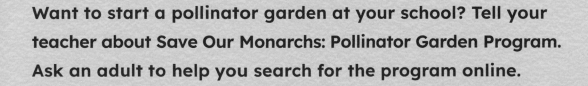

Want to start a pollinator garden at your school? Tell your teacher about Save Our Monarchs: Pollinator Garden Program. Ask an adult to help you search for the program online.

LEARN MORE

Creative Homeowner. *World of Pollinators: A Guide for All Explorers*. Mount Joy, PA: Creative Homeowner, 2023.

Hirsch, Rebecca E. *The Monarchs Are Missing: A Butterfly Mystery*. Minneapolis, MN: Millbrook Press, 2018.

London, Martha. *Pollinators: Animals Helping Plants Thrive*. Minneapolis, MN: ABDO, 2020.

Morlock, Rachael. *Be Smart About Antibiotics, Pesticides, and Hormones*. New York, NY: Cavendish Square, 2023.

GLOSSARY

agriculture (AA-grih-kuhl-chuhr) the business of how people grow crops

conservation (kahn-suhr-VAY-shuhn) action to protect wildlife and nature

crisis (KRY-suhss) a very difficult time or emergency

ecosystems (EE-koh-sih-stuhms) places where plants, animals, and the environment rely on each other

erosion (ih-ROH-zhuhn) when land is worn away by wind or water

extinction (ik-STINK-shuhn) when all of one kind of plant or animal die

grasslands (GRASS-lands) ecosystems of native grasses and wildflowers

habitat (hah-BUH-tat) the natural home of plants and animals

monocultures (MAH-nuh-kuhl-chuhrz) huge fields with one type of crop

native plants (NAY-tiv PLANTZ) plants that are a natural part of an ecosystem

organic (or-GAH-nik) food or other plants grown without toxic chemicals

pesticides (PEH-stuh-sydes) toxic chemicals made to kill a plant or animal that might harm crops

pollination (pah-luh-NAY-shuhn) moving pollen between flowers to help plants make new seeds

pollinators (PAH-luh-nay-tuhrz) animals that move pollen between plants

toxic (TAK-sik) something that is harmful or poisonous

INDEX